Alex Ferguson

CONTENTS

ALEX FERGUSON:
In a League of His Own

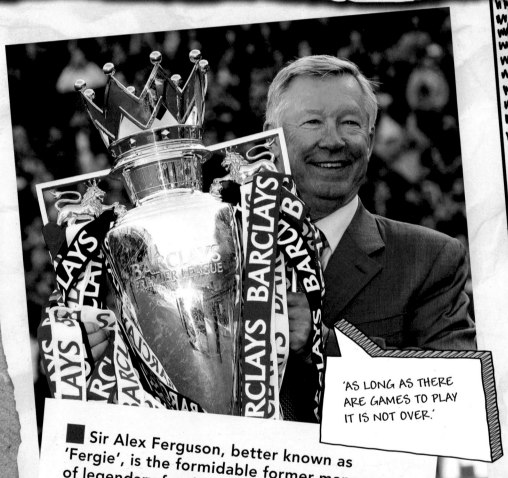

'AS LONG AS THERE ARE GAMES TO PLAY IT IS NOT OVER.'

■ Sir Alex Ferguson, better known as 'Fergie', is the formidable former manager of legendary football club Manchester United. As a manager, Fergie became famous for the careful management of his players and his determination to keep United at the top of the Premier League. During the course of his 26-year career with United, he helped the club to win an impressive string of trophies.

NAME: Alexander Ferguson

BORN: 31 December 1941

HOMETOWN: Glasgow, Scotland

HEIGHT: 1.8 metres (5 ft 9 inches)

MOTHER AND FATHER: Alexander Beaton Ferguson and Elizabeth Hardie

SCHOOLS: Broomloan Road Primary School and Govan High School

OCCUPATION: Former football player and football manager

FAMOUS FOR: Being the manager of Manchester United for 26 years

Old Trafford, Manchester United's home ground.

The North Stand was renamed after Fergie in 2011.

LEARNING THE HARD WAY

Fergie has had an extremely successful career, and is today a multi-millionaire, but he comes from ordinary roots. He was born into a working class family in Govan, an area in the Scottish city of Glasgow, on 31 December 1941.

FERGIE, SPEAKING ABOUT HIS CHILDHOOD: 'IT WAS A GREAT UPBRINGING. ALL WE EVER DID WAS PLAY FOOTBALL AND FIGHT. THAT'S WHAT YOU DID IN THESE AREAS.'

Fergie's father was a shipbuilder and his mother worked as a shop assistant. Just a year after Alex was born, his younger brother Martin joined the family. The Fergusons lived in a tenement, which is a large building split into separate flats. The family's home was simple, with only a metal tub in the living room for a bath.

FERGIE, SPEAKING ABOUT HIS UPBRINGING: 'YOU NEVER HAD A LOT, BUT I WOULDN'T CALL IT POVERTY. YOU ALWAYS HAD YOUR MEALS, YOU NEVER MISSED SCHOOL, YOU WERE ALWAYS CLEAN AND TIDY.'

While their parents were working, Fergie and his brother were often looked after by their grandparents. They also spent much of their time playing football on the streets of Govan with their friends, and fighting with the local gangs. Alex claims that his determination to succeed is down to his tough upbringing.

Drumchapel Amateurs in 1956.
Fergie is in the front row, third from left.

While at school, Fergie played football for the Life Boys and the Boys' Brigade, which were both youth groups for boys. He also joined the Drumchapel Amateurs club, for amateur footballers, many of whom later became professionals. As a youngster, Fergie's favourite football club was the Scottish club Glasgow Rangers, and he followed their games with a passion.

The emblem of Glasgow Rangers – Fergie's favourite team as a boy.

In 1957, at the age of 16, Fergie decided to leave school and began an apprenticeship making tools at a company called Wickman's, in Glasgow. At the same time, he also started playing football with Queen's Park, Scotland's most successful amateur football club.

FERGIE FACT!
FERGIE'S FATHER WAS A FIRM SUPPORTER OF THE LABOUR PARTY AND FERGIE LATER FOLLOWED SUIT – DETERMINED TO HELP THE PARTY THAT REPRESENTED WORKING CLASS PEOPLE, JUST LIKE HIMSELF AND HIS FAMILY.

Finding his FOOTBALL FEET

In his early career with Queen's Park, Fergie proved to be a good striker, but he was not regularly chosen to play for the team during matches. Fergie soon became frustrated that his football career was not progressing quickly. He often complained that the team's training was not good, or hard, enough. The tough attitude that he would later have as a manager was starting to show through!

FERGIE FACT!

IT WAS WHILE FERGIE WAS WORKING AS A TOOLMAKER THAT HE MET HIS FUTURE WIFE, CATHY HOLDING. HE HAD LIKED CATHY SINCE MEETING HER AT THE FACTORY WHERE THEY WORKED, AND WHEN HE SAW HER AT A DANCE ONE EVENING IN GLASGOW, HE DECIDED TO ASK HER OUT. THEIR RELATIONSHIP BLOSSOMED, AND THEY WENT ON TO MARRY.

Fergie's frustrations became so strong that at one point, he even considered emigrating to Canada to improve his life opportunities. However, things changed when he was approached by a scout from another club, St Johnstone FC, who promised the young footballer a regular place on the team.

Fergie playing for Dunfermline Athletic in 1965.

Fergie transferred to St Johnstone in 1960 and began training with the club in the evenings, while still holding down his apprenticeship by day. St Johnstone was in the city of Perth, and Fergie's day became a lot longer and more tiring because he now had to travel from Glasgow to Perth to train for the club. His daily routine often involved getting up at 6.45am to go to work, working a full day and then leaving at 4pm to go to Perth and train with St Johnstone. Fergie would train all evening and then travel home to Glasgow, not arriving until after midnight.

In 1964, the football club Dunfermline Athletic asked Fergie to join them, and he quickly signed up. After a few months with the club, he decided to become a full-time footballer and gave up his job as a toolmaker. With Dunfermeline, Fergie's football career went from strength to strength, and during the 1965-66 season, he scored a staggering 45 goals in 51 games.

Fergie's transfer from St Johnstone to Dunfermline and his decision to turn professional changed his life in many ways. His daily routine became much less strenuous and his journey to work more pleasant.

'...TO GET MY FIRST CAR AND BE ABLE TO DRIVE OVER TO DUMFERMLINE IN THE FRESH AIR EVERY MORNING – WHAT A DIFFERENCE!'

Family Man and RANGERS

FERGIE, SPEAKING ABOUT HIS FIRST SIGHTING OF CATHY: 'SHE WAS PRETTY, HAD A LOVELY WALK.. AND I MADE IT MY BUSINESS TO FIND OUT THAT SHE WAS CATHY HOLDING FROM TORYGLEN, NEAR HAMPDEN.'

In 1966, Cathy and Fergie married in Glasgow and moved into a house in the Simshill district of the city. The couple was married on a Saturday morning, and that afternoon, Fergie went to play in a match for Dunfermline! Fergie's success with Dunfermline soon brought him to the attention of his favourite childhood club, Rangers, who bought the talented player for £65,000 in 1967.

Happily settled into married life, and with his career on the rise, Fergie and Cathy started a family. Their son, Mark, was born in 1968 followed by twin boys, Jason and Darren, in 1972. Cathy stayed at home to look after the children while Fergie continued to play football for Rangers.

Fergie, Cathy and twin sons Jason and Darren in 1977.

Fergie may have liked Cathy from the moment he saw her, but Cathy's first impressions of Fergie were not good! She told her friend: 'Look at him – he looks a right bad yin [one]!' Fortunately, the footballer managed to win her around!

FERGIE FACT!

IN THE EARLY YEARS OF HIS MARRIAGE, WHILE ALSO PLAYING FOOTBALL, FERGIE RAN A PUB IN GLASGOW, WHICH HE NAMED 'FERGIE'S'!

Fergie

Despite his love for Rangers, Fergie's career with the club did not go as well as he had hoped. He was blamed for conceding a goal in the 1969 Scottish Cup Final when Rangers lost 4-0 to arch rivals Celtic. Ferguson left the club shortly after the defeat, and it was a disappointing end to the career he had hoped for with the club of his dreams.

Determined to still make a success of playing football, Fergie joined Falkirk in 1969. Realising that football careers are short, and recognising his ability to plan strategies and train players, Fergie now set his sights on coaching as well as playing. He was made the player-coach of the club, which meant that he played for the team and coached them, too.

Fergie's career took another downward turn, however, and after four seasons with the club, he was asked to leave by the new manager.

Hanging Up His Football Boots

After leaving Falkirk, Fergie played for Ayr United for a short time before he decided to retire as a player in 1974.

Fergie's career as a footballer might have been over, but his glittering career as a manager was just about to begin. In 1974, almost as soon as he finished playing for Ayr, and despite his young age, Fergie was offered the role of part-time manager for the club East Stirlingshire. He did not stay long in the job, and after managing the club for a short time, he moved to St Mirren.

Fergie found his coaching feet at St Mirren, and stayed there from 1974 to 1978. Under his vision and leadership, the club flourished, and was promoted to the First Division.

'WELL, FOOTBALL IS A HARD GAME; THERE'S NO DENYING IT. IT'S A GAME THAT CAN BRING OUT THE WORST IN YOU, AT TIMES.'

However, in 1978, things turned sour once more for Fergie when he was sacked by St Mirren. The club said that he had allowed his players to take payments that were not allowed. He was also accused of having entered into talks with Aberdeen about managing the club. It was a bitter end to what had seemed a successful role.

However, Fergie did not stay down for long! After his contract with St Mirren ended, Fergie took up the role of manager at Aberdeen, where he stayed until 1986. Under his leadership, the club did very well, and in 1980 Aberdeen won their first league title since 1955. With Fergie at the helm, the team went on to other victories, including the European Cup Winners' Cup in 1983.

'I'VE NEVER PLAYED FOR A DRAW IN MY LIFE.'

FERGIE FACT!

AT ST MIRREN, FERGIE GOT A REPUTATION FOR BEING A GREAT MANAGER – STRICT, BUT SOMEONE WHO GOT RESULTS. HE WAS KNOWN FOR EXPECTING PLAYERS TO FOLLOW HIS RULE AS LAW. IF THEY DID NOT, THEY WERE QUICKLY REPRIMANDED AND FELT THE FULL FORCE OF FERGIE'S RAGE. AS A RESULT, HE EARNED THE NICKNAME 'FURIOUS FERGUSON'!

JOINING THE RED DEVILS

By 1986, Fergie was riding high as a football manager and his career was rocketing. The spotlight was now firmly on him, and a number of top clubs asked him to join them as manager. However, it was Manchester United, also known as the Red Devils, which captured his imagination.

When Manchester United offered Fergie the role of manager in November 1986, he took up their offer and quickly made his mark. His strict rules and method of bringing in new, talented players, such as Steve Bruce, Brian McClair, Neil Webb and Paul Ince, slowly started to change the club and put it on the path to success.

Between 1986 and 1990, United improved steadily. However, things took a turn for the worse in September 1989 when United lost 5–1 to their great local rival, Manchester City. Some fans even began calling for Fergie to step down. Fergie held his nerve, though, and stayed focused on his vision for the club he had come to love.

'I HAVE ALWAYS TRIED TO BE THE BRIDGE BETWEEN THE CLUB AND THE FANS AND I HAVE TRIED TO SUPPORT THE FANS IN A LOT OF THEIR PLEAS AND CAUSES.'

Fergie's determination to ride out the storm won through when United won the FA Cup at the end of the season. Spurred on by his success, Fergie looked to add more new, talented players to the United team. He set his sights on Eric Cantona, a player who was signed to Leeds United. Fergie bought Cantona and added him to the United line-up in 1992. The buy paid off, and United won their first league title in 1992.

Fergie leads United out at the FA Cup Final in 1990.

FERGIE FACT!

ERIC CANTONA HAD A STRONG WORK ETHIC THAT WAS MUCH LIKE FERGIE'S OWN. AFTER TRAINING, CANTONA WOULD ASK FERGIE IF HE COULD STAY ON TO PRACTICE WITH TWO OTHER PLAYERS. FERGIE WAS IMPRESSED BY THE FOOTBALLER'S DRIVE, AND GAVE HIM NOT TWO BUT THREE PLAYERS TO HELP WITH HIS EXTRA PRACTICE.

FERGIE ON CANTONA: 'IF EVER THERE WAS ONE PLAYER, ANYWHERE IN THE WORLD, THAT WAS MADE FOR MANCHESTER UNITED, IT WAS CANTONA. HE SWAGGERED IN, STUCK HIS CHEST OUT, RAISED HIS HEAD AND SURVEYED EVERYTHING AS THOUGH HE WERE ASKING: "I'M CANTONA. HOW BIG ARE YOU? ARE YOU BIG ENOUGH FOR ME?"'

RED VICTORY

The Reds were now on the rise – and so was Fergie. The superstar coach became ever more popular among United fans and his reputation as a great manager spread. Fergie's hard work and dedication was starting to pay off.

In 1994, United won both the Premier League and the FA Cup. Then, in 1999, they became the first team to win the Premier League, FA Cup and UEFA Champions League – 'The Treble' – in the same season. This brought them global fame. United and Fergie were now the team and coach to watch. United became one of the richest football clubs in the world.

Between 1993 and 2013, under Fergie's leadership and determination, Manchester United were incredibly successful. Their wins included a vast number of league titles and cups.

Fergie lifts the FA Cup aloft in May 1999.

Fergie's Biggest Wins

Teddy Sheringham and David Beckham lift the UEFA Champions League trophy in 1999, after beating Bayern Munich 2-1.

Premier League (13):

1992–93	1993–94	1995–96
1996–97	1998–99	1999–2000
2000–01	2002–03	2006–07
2007–08	2008–09	2010–11
2012–13		

FA Cup (5):

1989–90	1993–94	1995–96
1998–99	2003–04	

League Cup (4):
1991–92, 2005–06, 2008–09, 2009–10.

Charity/Community Shield (10):

1990	1993	1994
1996	1997	2003
2007	2008	2010
2011		

UEFA Champions League (2):

1998–99	2007–08

UEFA Cup Winners' Cup (1):
1990–91

UEFA Super Cup (1):
1991

FERGIE ON WINNING THE 1999 UEFA CHAMPIONS LEAGUE:
I CAN'T BELIEVE IT. I CAN'T BELIEVE IT. FOOTBALL...!'

Intercontinental Cup (1):
1999

FIFA Club World Cup (1):
2008

FERGIE RULES!

Fergie is known in football for his fiery personality and clashes with journalists, other managers and footballers. People who worked with the headstrong manager have said he sometimes lost his temper, and even kicked tea urns and football boots at players during half time if they were not performing as he wanted.

However, despite his fiery outbursts, Fergie's players have always had enormous respect for and a huge sense of loyalty towards their manager. Fergie's leadership and vision for his sport have had such a huge influence on his players that some, such as Ryan Giggs and Paul Scholes, have spent their entire careers at Manchester United, under his guidance and leadership.

FERGIE ON WAYNE ROONEY'S TRANSFER REQUEST: 'SOMETIMES YOU LOOK IN A FIELD AND YOU SEE A COW AND YOU THINK IT'S A BETTER COW THAN THE ONE YOU'VE GOT IN YOUR OWN FIELD. IT'S A FACT. RIGHT? AND IT NEVER REALLY WORKS OUT THAT WAY.'

Many top players, such as David Beckham, say that Fergie helped them to shape their early football careers. They believe that without Fergie's guiding hand and strict routine, they would have struggled to stay focussed on the game and might well have gone off the rails at a young age.

Under Fergie's leadership, some of the greatest football players in modern times have played for Manchester United, including Eric Cantona, Ryan Giggs, David Beckham, Cristiano Ronaldo and Wayne Rooney.

Beckham playing for LA Galaxy in 2011.

FERGIE ON RONALDO: 'CRISTIANO RONALDO WAS THE MOST GIFTED PLAYER I MANAGED. HE SURPASSED ALL THE OTHER GREAT ONES I COACHED AT UNITED.'

FERGIE FACT!

FERGIE'S LEGENDARY BAD TEMPER IS SAID TO HAVE BEEN BEHIND THE CUT THAT APPEARED ON DAVID BECKHAM'S FACE IN 2003. HE ALLEGEDLY KICKED A FOOTBALL BOOT INTO BECKHAM'S FACE, ALTHOUGH FERGIE HAS SINCE SAID IT WAS AN ACCIDENT: 'IT WAS A FREAKISH INCIDENT. IF I TRIED IT 100 OR A MILLION TIMES IT COULDN'T HAPPEN AGAIN. IF I COULD I WOULD HAVE CARRIED ON PLAYING!'

Ryan Giggs

FERGIE ON RYAN GIGGS: 'I REMEMBER THE FIRST TIME I SAW HIM. HE WAS 13 AND JUST FLOATED OVER THE GROUND LIKE A COCKER SPANIEL CHASING A PIECE OF SILVER PAPER IN THE WIND.'

WINNING BIG

'THE CULMINATION OF THREE TROPHIES WAS THE PINNACLE OF MY CAREER AND IT HAS BEEN REWARDED WITH A KNIGHTHOOD.'

Amazing facts and figures show just how incredible Fergie's career was. Here are some of his greatest achievements, including many triumphs with the Red Devils, and some of his own words about his success:

49
THE NUMBER OF TROPHIES WON BY FERGIE AS MANAGER OF MANCHESTER UNITED, ABERDEEN AND ST MIRREN.

26
THE NUMBER OF YEARS UNITED HAD GONE WITHOUT A LEAGUE TITLE BEFORE FERGIE HELPED THE CLUB TO VICTORY IN 1993.

104
THE NUMBER OF PLAYERS FERGIE SIGNED WHILE AT UNITED.

'IF MY PARENTS WERE STILL ALIVE, THEY WOULD BE VERY PROUD. THEY GAVE ME A GOOD START IN LIFE, THE VALUES THAT HAVE DRIVEN ME, AND THE CONFIDENCE TO BELIEVE IN MYSELF.'

'IT'S ... IMPORTANT THAT UNITED ARE THE BEST TEAM IN THE COUNTRY IN TERMS OF WINNING TITLES.'

FERGIE FACT!

FERGIE EARNED A REPORTED £5 MILLION A YEAR BY THE END OF HIS CAREER WITH UNITED.

13
THE NUMBER OF PREMIER LEAGUE TITLES WON BY THE REDS UNDER FERGIE.

1,498
THE NUMBER OF GAMES PLAYED BY UNITED THAT FERGIE OVERSAW.

2,045
THE NUMBER OF POINTS WON IN THE PREMIER LEAGUE BY UNITED UNDER FERGIE.

9-0
THE BIGGEST UNITED WIN UNDER FERGIE – AGAINST IPSWICH TOWN IN 1995.

During his career at United, Fergie often made headline news – either for run-ins with his players or his outspoken views when interviewed by journalists. The football coach made both friends and enemies among other football managers, too. Some of his feuds with managers and journalists lasted for years, including his famous fights with Arsène Wenger and Rafael Benítez.

Rafael Benítez

FERGIE ON RAFAEL BENÍTEZ: 'HE IS VERY CONCERNED ABOUT HIS CV. HE REFERS TO IT QUITE A LOT.'

As a coach, Fergie had strong beliefs about how football should be played and a steely determination to make sure that his team won – even if that meant questioning the rulings of football officials. Referees were often in Fergie's firing line, and he never hesitated to challenge them about their decisions during matches. Fergie's head-on attacks and heated outbursts sometimes led to him appearing before FA disciplinary panels to explain his behaviour.

FERGIE ON MANCHESTER CITY: 'SOMETIMES YOU HAVE A NOISY NEIGHBOUR. YOU CANNOT DO ANYTHING ABOUT THAT. THEY WILL ALWAYS BE NOISY. YOU JUST HAVE TO GET ON WITH YOUR LIFE, PUT YOUR TELEVISION ON AND TURN IT UP A BIT LOUDER.'

FERGIE ON SELLING CRISTIANO RONALDO TO REAL MADRID: 'DO YOU THINK I WOULD ENTER INTO A CONTRACT WITH THAT MOB? ABSOLUTELY NO CHANCE. I WOULD NOT SELL THEM A VIRUS. THAT IS A 'NO' BY THE WAY. THERE IS NO AGREEMENT WHATSOEVER BETWEEN THE CLUBS.'

Fergie was always happy to share his thoughts about his fellow managers and other clubs in public. He was even accused of playing mind games to put off other managers and their players before a big match or during an ongoing championship. Whatever tactics Fergie used, his aim was always clear – to make sure that United won.

FERGIE FACT!

FERGIE AND RAFAEL BENÍTEZ FIRST CLASHED WHEN BENÍTEZ FIRST TOOK CONTROL OF LIVERPOOL IN 2004. FERGIE SAID THAT BY ACCUSING HIM OF BREAKING FOOTBALL RULES AND GETTING AWAY WITH IT, BENÍTEZ HAD CROSSED THE LINE – AND IN DOING SO HAD CHANGED FERGIE'S ATTITUDE TOWARDS HIM FOREVER: 'ONCE YOU MADE IT PERSONAL, YOU HAD NO CHANCE, BECAUSE I COULD WAIT. I HAD SUCCESS ON MY SIDE. BENÍTEZ WAS STRIVING FOR TROPHIES WHILE ALSO TAKING ME ON. THAT WAS UNWISE.'

Nobody Better

Fergie stands out as a truly great football manager for many reasons. He stayed at the top of his game – and he made sure that his players did, too. Fergie got to know his players inside out. He made sure that he knew their weaknesses and their strengths, and then played on these to the game's advantage.

FERGIE ON DAVID BECKHAM:
'DAVID WAS THE ONLY PLAYER I MANAGED WHO CHOSE TO BE FAMOUS.'

'DAVID THOUGHT HE WAS BIGGER THAN FERGUSON. THERE IS NO DOUBT ABOUT THAT IN MY MIND.'

Fergie also understood that a player was never bigger than the team, and he let them know it. Even football superstars such as David Beckham were not too great for Fergie. When Beckham started to clash with Fergie, he let him know firmly who was boss, and that the team came before any individual player.

FERGIE FACT!

DESPITE FERGIE'S GREAT SUCCESS AS MANAGER OF UNITED, HE WAS NEVER TEMPTED TO BE MANAGER OF ENGLAND AND TURNED DOWN TWO OFFERS TO TAKE UP THE ROLE, SAYING: 'THERE WAS NO WAY I COULD CONTEMPLATE THAT. IT WASN'T A BED OF NAILS I WAS EVER TEMPTED TO LIE ON.'

SEPP BLATTER, PRESIDENT OF FIFA, ON FERGIE: 'WHAT IS EXTRAORDINARY IS THAT IN TODAY'S WORLD, IN WHICH COACHES ARE EXPECTED TO PRODUCE INSTANT RESULTS OR BE CHANGED, HIS LONGEVITY IS A SHINING EXAMPLE OF WHAT CAN BE ACHIEVED THROUGH STABILITY, CONTINUITY, TRUST AND CONFIDENCE IN ONE PERSONALITY.'

Fergie was determined to manage his team without interference and did not bend when he came under criticism. He had both a vision for success and the will to make it happen.

His enormous contribution to the world of football was recognised by the football governing body, FIFA, at an awards ceremony in 2012. There, Fergie was given the President's Award for his work as manager of United. The award was presented by the FIFA President Sepp Blatter, who said of Fergie: 'Football is all about winning games and titles, and there is nobody better than him.'

Alex Ferguson presents Ryan Giggs with the BBC Wales Sports Personality of the Year award in 2009.

25

GOODBYE, United

Fergie was still in charge of Manchester United as his 65th birthday drew near. People started to talk about when the unbeatable manager would finally think about retiring. However, Fergie showed no signs of slowing down or of giving up his leadership of the Reds.

Despite his age, the extraordinary manager was more passionate than ever about the game and as determined to win every match that United played. Fergie continued to build what seemed an unstoppable team and looked to the future for ever more glorious victories.

Fergie holds his autobiography, which was published in 2013.

'I THINK IT'S IMPORTANT TO WORK AND I'M ENTITLED TO WORK. SOME PEOPLE DO NOT WANT TO WORK BUT I WANT TO CONTINUE WORKING.'

ALEX FERGUSON

MY AUTOBIOGRAPHY

Fergie continued to lead United into football battles and victories until 2013, when he decided it was finally time to call it a day. He told his much-loved club, and then the world, that he was stepping down from his role and retiring – at the age of 72. Fergie felt that he had taken the club to a point at which it was truly great and strong, and that it was now time to let someone else take over: 'It was important to me to leave an organisation in the strongest possible shape and I believe I have done so.'

ON RETIREMENT, FERGIE PAID TRIBUTE TO HIS PLAYERS AND TEAM FOR THEIR HARD WORK DURING HIS TIME AT UNITED:

'AS FOR MY PLAYERS AND STAFF, PAST AND PRESENT, I WOULD LIKE TO THANK THEM ALL FOR A STAGGERING LEVEL OF PROFESSIONAL CONDUCT AND DEDICATION THAT HAS HELPED TO DELIVER SO MANY MEMORABLE TRIUMPHS. WITHOUT THEIR CONTRIBUTION THE HISTORY OF THIS GREAT CLUB WOULD NOT BE AS RICH.'

Fergie ended his amazing career on a high by watching his club win its 13th Premier League title. It was a moment of great joy and pride for the tireless manager.

When Fergie finally retired, many in the world of football said it was unlikely they would ever again see another manager of his determination, skill and devotion to the game.

How do you score on FERGIE?

By now you should know a lot about Alex Ferguson. Test your knowledge of him by answering these questions:

1 Where was Fergie born?
a) Glasgow
b) London
c) Oxford

2 What is the name of Fergie's brother?
a) Mark
b) Christopher
c) Martin

3 Which political party does Fergie support?
a) Labour
b) Conservative
c) Liberal Democrat

4 What was Fergie's favourite childhood football club?
a) Manchester United
b) Glasgow Rangers
c) Arsenal

5 How old was Fergie when he retired as a professional player?
a) 27
b) 36
c) 32

6 In what year did United have their first FA Cup win under Fergie?
a) 1990
b) 1989
c) 1995

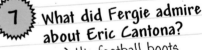

7 What did Fergie admire about Eric Cantona?
a) His football boots
b) His understanding of the game
c) His strong work ethic

8 What did Fergie allegedly kick at David Beckham's face?
a) A football boot
b) A tea cup
c) A football

9 How many times did United win the Premier League under Fergie?
   a) 10 times
   b) 11 times
   c) 13 times

10 Who did Fergie consider to be the greatest football player he had ever coached?
   a) Cristiano Ronaldo
   b) David Beckham
   c) Wayne Rooney

ANSWERS

1 a) Glasgow
2 c) Martin
3 a) Labour
4 b) Glasgow Rangers
5 c) 32
6 a) 1990
7 c) His strong work ethic
8 a) A football boot
9 c) 13 times
10 a) Cristiano Ronaldo

Find out more about United:

Books
Big Business: Manchester United by Adam Sutherland (Wayland, 2014)

Websites
Read the story of Fergie's life at:
www.siralexferguson.net

Quote sources
Page 4 The Daily Mail, 2012; **Page 6** (top) Daily Record, 2013, (bottom) Patrick Barclay, 2010; **Page 9** Patrick Barclay, 2010; **Page 11** Daily Mail, 2013; **Page 12** Shortlist.com; **Page 13** The Daily Mail, 2013; **Page 14** The Daily Telegraph, 2004; **Page 15** Shortlist.com; **Page 16** The Daily Mail, 2011; **Page 18** The Mirror, 2013; **Page 19** (top) The Metro, 2013, (bottom) The Independent, 2014; **Page 20** BBC News, 1999; **Page 21** (bottom) BBC News, 2011, (top) The Daily Mail, 2012; **Page 22** The Independent, 2013; **Page 23** (top) The Independent, 2014, (middle) The Independent, 2008, (bottom) The Independent, 2013; **Page 24** (top) BBC News, 2014, (middle) The Guardian, 2013, (bottom) The Evening Times, 2013; **Page 25** The Guardian, 2013; **Page 26** The Daily Mail, 2012; **Page 27** (left) BBC News, 2013, (right) Daily Mail, 2013

GLOSSARY

amateur
A footballer who is not paid to play for a club

apprenticeship
A training position in a workplace in order to learn a trade

conduct
The way a person behaves

contemplate
To think about something

continuity
A seamless flow between one thing and another

devoted
Completely committed

disciplinary
Punishing or reprimanding

district
Part of a city

emigrating
Leaving your home country to live abroad

football governing body
An organisation of people who make decisions about the game

formidable
Having great strength

headstrong
Determined, believing that your ideas are the best ones

humble
Modest

knighthood
A title the Queen gives to a person who has shown exceptional skills or behaviour

longevity
A long period of time

loyalty
To stay true to, or stand by, someone or something

officials
People who have been given a position of authority

outburst
Speaking out with passion

pleas
Requests for help

poverty
A situation in which a person has very little money

professional
A footballer who is paid to play for a club

reprimanded
Told off

INDEX